THE STORY OF
Saint Columba

"Master, it is not safe. Let us go back."

"We will be killed by these wild people."

"Turn back while there is still time."

"They have spears in their hands. Perhaps if we turn back now, they will let us go."

The man in the monk's robe did not reply. He walked on in front, a tall staff in his hand. The narrow path wound in and out of the trees by the banks of a wide, swift river. His followers looked fearfully around them. There were only a few of them, with satchels on their backs. One led two ponies roped together. Bags containing their food and a few belongings were slung on each side of the ponies. Through the trees and bushes they could see other people – fierce-looking men wearing animal skins, with painted faces. They had spears and cudgels, and they moved silently through the trees, always keeping pace with the travellers.

As the monk and his followers walked on, the number of watchers grew more and more. They still made no sound, but this only made the monk's followers more worried. Then finally the little group came to a place where the path ran right down to the water's edge and stopped.

THE STORY OF
Saint
COLUMBA

CORBIE

Text by David Ross
Illustrated by Mike Lacey, Simon Girling and Associates

© 1998 Waverley Books Ltd
Reprinted 1999

Published by Waverley Books Ltd,
New Lanark, Scotland

ISBN 1 902407 04 0

Printed and bound in Indonesia

Across the river they could see where it began again on the other side.

Also on the other side, a little boat was tied to a stake driven into the bank.

"Lugneus Macumin," said the monk to one of his followers. "We will need that boat. You are the best swimmer. Will you swim across and bring it over to us?"

"Oh, master," said Lugneus. "I will surely drown. See how fast the river runs, and how deep and dark the water is. I am afraid to cross."

"You will not drown. No harm shall befall you," said the monk. He looked around him. The spear-carriers were coming closer and closer, but he paid no attention to them.

With a sulky, frightened face, Lugneus pulled off his tunic, stepped down into the water and began to swim. He struck out for the far side, but just as he reached the middle of the river, something terrifying happened.

A huge head rose out of the water on a long green neck. Tangled fronds of hair or weed hung down from it. Its jaws opened wide, showing huge teeth, and its green eyes gleamed as it bent its neck to bite at Lugneus. The spearmen rushed to the bank and gave a great shout of fear and wonder.

"Help!" called Lugneus pitifully. He floundered in the water, the monster rearing above him.

Then the monk took two steps forward until his feet were in the water. Raising his arm, he made a great sign in the air with an outstretched finger – a down-stroke followed by a shorter stroke across it. To his followers it seemed as if in that breathless moment a real cross hung in the air before them.

"Begone," cried the monk in a voice that made the ground shake. "In the name of the Saviour, I command you, return to the depths!"

The huge creature swung furiously towards him, but the monk did not move back. Gripping his staff, he stood facing it. For a moment it seemed that the beast was going to turn on him. Then suddenly the monster fell back into the water with a hiss and a mighty splash, and the swirling waters closed over it. The terrified Lugneus was drifting away on the river.

"Go on, Lugneus," called the monk. "Swim hard. Fetch the boat. Did I not say you would not be harmed?"

The spearmen were gaping at him with amazement and fear. The monster that had so long terrified them had been defeated by this one man. He stepped back on to the path and stood in front of them. They no longer looked dangerous. They bowed deeply to him, as they might have done to a king.

They were Picts, the people who lived in Scotland more than a thousand years ago. Some of them might have been your ancestors, but you would have to put the word "great" about a hundred times in front of the word "grandfather" to get anywhere near them. The monk was on his way to visit their king. The dark river was the River Ness, and they were close to the place we now call Inverness.

The monk's name was Colum Cille or Kil. That means "dove of the church", and we know of him as Saint Columba. The story of Columba and the monster is a very old one, but even today there are people who believe there is a monster that lives in the depths of Loch Ness.

Columba was a missionary. He had come to tell the Picts about Jesus Christ and to persuade them to become Christians. There was only one way to do that, and that was to get their king to become a Christian. Then his people would follow. The king of the Picts was called Brude.

Columba did not know what Brude would say or do, but he knew he had to try to persuade the king.

The king's fortress was on the top of a hill. It was surrounded by a high wooden wall, and the gates were shut. King Brude knew by now that Columba was coming, but he did not want to see him. Standing in front of the closed gates, C o l u m b a again raised his arm. Again he made the  sign of the cross. The barred gates flew open before him, and he walked in, his followers keeping very close behind him. The king of the Picts came out of his house, with his warriors around him. Also with him were the druids, the priests of the Pictish people. They hated Columba, not just because of his teachings but also because if the king became a Christian they would no longer be important. It was a tense moment.

"We will all be killed," thought Lugneus again, but then he looked at the calm face of his master, Columba, and thought, "This man can do anything."

In the old story, it was told that Columba succeeded in his aim and that Brude became a Christian that very day. We know now that it did not happen like that. But Brude did listen to what Columba said and agreed that he could go anywhere he liked in the kingdom of the Picts. The druids were very angry because they saw their king had become the missionary's friend. And in the end, King Brude and the Picts did become Christians.

Columba had come to King Brude from Iona, a tiny island off the west coast of Scotland. There he had built a church. In those days, most of the people who lived in Scotland and England and Wales were not Christians. Columba, and the friends who came to join him on Iona, wanted to make them Christians and wanted them to live in peace instead of always fighting.

Columba knew all about fighting. As a young man he had been the cause of a great battle. He was born and grew up in Ireland. His family was an important one, and even when he was a little boy, he was used to getting his own way. The people of Ireland were Christians. While he was still a young child, Columba was put into the care of a priest, and it was at this time he was given the name of Colum of the Church. As Columba grew older, he decided to become a monk. He was sent to the monastery of Clonard, whose abbot was Finnian. Then he went on to found monasteries himself. One of these was at Durrow, which became famous for its beautiful illustrated books. Columba encouraged his monks to write these books – Bible stories with coloured letters and many pictures. Every book had to be written by hand, which took a long time, so they were rare and precious. Finnian of Clonard had a splendid

one with the Psalms written down in it, which he kept in his study.

The young Columba saw this book and thought it was wonderful. He wished he had a copy of it. At last, he wanted it so badly that he went secretly into Finnian's study and began to copy the book. Night after night he worked until it was almost complete. But Finnian caught him at it and was very angry.

"You had no right to copy my book without asking me," he said.

"But I have not harmed your book," replied Columba. "I only copied it."

"The copy belongs to me. Hand it over," said the abbot.

But Columba refused to give it up. So Finnian complained to the king, Diarmid. Diarmid was the king of Finnian's people but not of Columba's. He listened to Finnian, and he listened to Columba. At last he gave his decision.

"Just as a calf goes with a cow, so a copy goes with the book it was taken from," he said. And Columba was made to give up the book.

Columba was very angry. Soon afterwards, he returned to his own people and urged them to make war against Diarmid. They assembled an army, and so did Diarmid. There was a fierce battle and many men were killed. After the battle, Columba got back his copy of Finnian's book, but he was in great trouble. The leaders of the church told him he had broken his vows as a monk. Monks all had to promise to be humble and obedient and to be men of peace. Columba was none of these things. He had been proud, disobedient and warlike. They wanted to make him leave the church. Columba was now deeply sorry for all the harm he had done. Luckily for him, among the great men of the church was Saint Brendan. He saw that Columba was truly sorry, and he believed that the young man could still do a great deal of good in the world. He asked the others for Columba to be given a new chance. In the end they agreed but said that Columba must leave Ireland for ever. Sadly, he left his Irish home, but he did not go far away.

Already some of Columba's people lived in the west of Scotland, just across the sea from Ireland. Their king, Conall, allowed Columba to come to Iona with twelve followers. Columba now worked as hard for peace and love as he had once done for war and hatred. Soon Iona became famous in the western world. Many young men came to join in

the work. And, although Columba did return to Ireland a few times, from then on Iona was his home, and he grew to love it, calling it "Iona of my heart".

While his relations in Ireland lived a rich life, Columba lived in a little hut close to the wooden buildings of his monastery. He slept not on a bed but on a stone slab. There was a little church, a hut where the monks all ate together, a food store, and the tiny huts of the monks. There was also a guest-house. Visitors often came. Some of them were other holy men from Scotland or Ireland. Some of them were kings or kings' messengers, for all the little kingdoms of that time were anxious to have Columba's advice. Whoever they were, Columba would wash their feet, as a sign that they were welcome and that he was their humble servant.

There were three things that Columba wanted to do in his lifetime. One was to teach more young men to be monks like himself. Another was to produce beautiful books, the coloured pages of which not only told the Bible story but praised God by their beauty and the hard work that had gone into their making. The third was to persuade all the people in Scotland to become Christians. Columba and other missionaries walked all over

Scotland, at a time when it was a wild and dangerous country, and often were in danger of being attacked or killed, but nothing could stop them.

Although he wanted only to work for God, Columba could not stop people asking his advice on other matters. Sometimes these were very important. One of his visits back to Ireland was with King Aidan, the successor to King Conall. At that time the king of Irish Dalriada was the overlord of Scottish Dalriada. Columba and Aidan were able to change this, so that no more tribute was paid to Ireland. In this way, Columba is one of the founders of the independent kingdom of Scotland.

On the level ground of the island of Iona, below the little hill of Dun-I, were the fields where the monks grew their crops and grazed their cows and sheep. Everything they ate came from their own fields and the surrounding sea. Milk from the cows was carried to the monastery by an old white horse, called by Columba "the faithful servant", and he would bless it as he passed it.

Columba was still hot-tempered, but now he took care not to let his temper get the better of him. When a man accused of killing seals that

belonged to the monastery was brought before him, he simply said, "Why did you not tell us that you were in need? We would have looked after you."

He and his monks often went without food. Their lives were hard. They wanted to show that they were as poor as Jesus and his disciples had been.

The time came when Columba was too old and weak to walk about any more. He was no longer able to climb the hill of Dun-I and look out across the sea to where Ireland lay, out of sight beyond the horizon. His monks made him a little chariot, and in this he would visit them as they worked in the fields. He had a faithful servant, Diormit, who looked after him, for the old man hardly troubled to take care of himself. One day in springtime, when wild primroses were peeping through the short grass, he said quietly to Diormit, "I have some words to say to you in secret, and you must promise to reveal them to no one else."

Diormit promised, and Columba said, "Today is Sunday, which is the day of rest from work. And it is the day when all my work will come to an end, and when I shall rest. At midnight of this holy day I will go to join my fathers."

Diormit wept, and Columba comforted him. As his servant helped him to walk along, the old white horse, the "faithful servant", came up and nuzzled him, and he gave it a final blessing. Somehow he found the strength to make a last climb of Dun-I and looked down from the top at the little cluster of huts and blessed it. He attended the evening service as usual, and then went back to his hut. But when the bell rang for midnight, he rose and went back to the little church. Now Diormit hurriedly called the monks together, and they rushed in, in time to see him raise his hand in a final blessing to them before he died.

Many great men would have come to his funeral, but for three days a great storm raged and no boat could reach Iona. So Columba was buried as he would have wished, and as he had lived, simply and plainly, with only the monks of Iona to bid him farewell.

I O N A   A F T E R   C O L U M B A

After the death of Columba, Iona was treated as a very holy place. Many people came to visit the saint's grave. Other holy men were buried there too, like Saint Adamnan who first wrote Columba's life story. For hundreds of years it was the burial place for Scottish kings. No fewer than forty-eight of them are buried there.

But those were also times of danger and disaster. The Vikings, raiding from Norway and Orkney, often invaded the island, stole its treasures and killed the monks. For a long time, Iona, like the other Western Isles, was not part of Scotland at all but was ruled by the King of Norway. After Scotland regained the Isles, the Abbey was rebuilt and enlarged as a fine stone building. In 1507 it became the Cathedral of the Isles. Monks and nuns lived there until the Reformation in 1561.

After that, the great church and the other buildings fell into disuse. For more than three hundred years they crumbled away, until in 1899 the Duke of Argyll, who by then was the owner of the island, presented the ruins to the Church of Scotland.

Restoration work began, and from 1910 church services were again held in the Abbey. Now the buildings are in the care of the Iona Community, founded by the Reverend George MacLeod. Once again, many pilgrims come to Iona, and today they come not just from Scotland but from countries all over the world.

SOME DATES FROM THE
LIFE OF SAINT COLUMBA

◆ Born at Gartan, County Donegal, 521

◆ Joins St Finnian's school, where he is ordained deacon, around 540

◆ Fights in battle 561

◆ Comes to Iona 563

◆ Visits King Brude 565

◆ Goes with King Aidan to Ireland 575

◆ Revisits Ireland, visiting monasteries which he had founded, around 585

◆ Dies on Iona, 597